MY AFTERLIFE
GUARANTEED

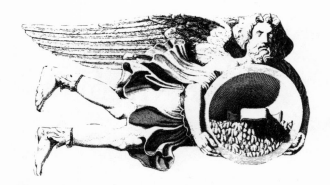

MY AFTERLIFE GUARANTEED

& Other Narratives

Nanos Valaoritis

City Lights Books
San Francisco

Acknowledgements:

Some of these narratives have been collected in these Greek publications of Nanos Valaoritis' work: *Central Arcade*, Athens, 1958; *Some Women*, Themelio Press, Athens, 1982; *Poems* (vol. I), Ypsilon Press, Athens, 1983; and *The Talking Monkey*, Aigokeros Press, Athens, 1986. In the United States, several poems and stories are from the author's books *Hired Hieroglyphs*, Kayak Press, Santa Cruz, 1970, and *Flash Bloom*, Wire Press, San Francisco, 1980. Other texts made their first appearance in *City Lights Review*, *Exquisite Corpse*, *Not Guilty*, *Pali*, and *Velocities*.

Cover design by: Dimitris Kalokyris
Book design by: Patricia Fujii

Library of Congress Cataloging-in-Publication Data

Valaoritis, Nanos.
        My afterlife guaranteed & other narratives   /   Nanos Valaoritis
              p.   cm.
        ISBN: 0-8726-248-8
        I. Title.   I. Title: My afterlife guaranteed and other narratives.
PS3572.A38M9   1990
813'.54—dc20

City Lights Books are available to bookstores through our primary distributor: Subterranean Company, P.O. Box 10233, Eugene, OR 97440. 1-503-343-6324. Toll free orders: 1-800-274-7826. Our books are also available through library jobbers and regional distributors. For personal orders and catalogs, write to City Lights Books, 261 Columbus Avenue, San Francisco, CA 94133.

CITY LIGHTS BOOKS are edited by Lawrence Ferlinghetti and Nancy J. Peters and published at the City Lights Bookstore, 261 Columbus Avenue, San Francisco, CA 94133.

TRANSLATORS

Written in Greek, the following were

Translated by Mary Kitroeff

>Three Problems of the Sea
>Hermes and Hermione
>Penthesileia
>The Black Sun
>The Way Things Go
>Coup d'Etat
>Procrustes
>The Triumph of Decadence

Translated by Lennart Bruce (from Swedish)

>Transubstantiation

Translated by Allegro Shartz

>Who We Are
>The Bride
>Gloomy Reality
>The Train
>The Tree of Happiness
>The Thieves
>The Windows of Genius
>The Games of the Circle

Translated by the author

>Borisofski's Lair
>How I Met Ionesco

The other narratives in this book were written in English.

CONTENTS

Procrustes

Procrustes was a great lover of the human body. He couldn't bear bodies that didn't fit the model he had in his mind. He had trained his eyes to pick up on even the slightest imperfection. Nothing escaped him. And then he would become merciless. He would crush and cut up all those that didn't conform. For this he had built a bed that fit only the body he had set as a measure.

The measurements had been calculated by him so precisely that it was impossible for someone to lie down if he didn't possess the required dimensions. And if that person didn't (and it was quite improbable that anyone would), too bad for him.

Since he not only had good taste but was also an excellent craftsman, he took immediate pains, with unbelievable patience and persistence, to improve upon the body that had fallen into his hands. He never let anyone go unless he had first remade him exactly the way he wanted. And this habit cost the lives of many who passed through his neck of the woods. Those who were too tall had their legs sawed off and even their heads sometimes if necessary. Those who were too short were stretched until they reached the length of the bed. We shouldn't get the wrong idea just because sometimes, well, I should really say always, the stretching would break the body in two and the poor wretch would die. Procrustes' motives were fine, beyond reproach. The fact that he kept failing wasn't his fault. It was the fault of those who are born so imperfectly. And so Procrustes lived with this passion quite unhappily, dreaming and hoping for at least one person who would fit, someone flawless who wouldn't disappoint him. Otherwise he would be doomed forever to keep trying, and to subject his guests to all sorts of tortures. And that would be deeply upsetting to both him and to them.

But fate rewarded him generously for all his trouble and sent him Theseus. As soon as he saw Theseus coming round the path with the sword and sandals of Aegeus and the terrible club hanging at his side, he was completely dumbfounded. He stood like that for a moment, not moving, just staring. The veins on his forehead bulged as he tried to control his emotion.

As white as a sheet and with his heart beating wildly he waited for the hero to approach. He couldn't believe his eyes. He thought the gods were teasing him and sending a ghost, a vision, so they could laugh at him.

"It can't be," he thought, shaking, "that such a body exists." And yet he wasn't wrong. The moment was great.

And Theseus kept coming closer without suspecting the agitation his presence had caused. He had heard about an ordeal which some evil man imposed on all passersby. But he hadn't paid much attention. He was so confident and sure of himself that nothing worried him. So he kept on walking at a steady pace and gazed scornfully at his inquisitor. Procrustes, on the other hand, once he had recovered from the shock, prepared to fight for his life. What took place, what was said between these two when they met, tradition will not say. So let us try to restore what ensued.

Procrustes was by no means a fool. He knew right away what he was up against and that his usual method was no longer adequate. So he abandoned all pretext from the start and invited the stranger to a duel. For his part Theseus could not be sure that if he accepted the invitation he would be the winner. And it is on this issue that commentators are sharply divided. One view is that Theseus' innocence was so great that it disarmed Procrustes and the bed, adjusting itself to the hero's measurements, abandoned its privilege of being invincible and eternally incompatible with anything human. This somewhat poetic interpretation is countered by a more cynical solution. It being that Procrustes' greatest weapon was the other person; the one who would undergo the test. Not only was the bed no different from any other, but it didn't even exist except in the imagination of the guest. Yet the conviction that it existed was so deeply rooted in him, that a perfectly innocent bed was transformed into a place of torture and suffering, with Procrustes hardly interfering at all. They say Theseus had been told this secret by the gods or that he was so completely unaware of it that he escaped the danger of a myth that endured all-powerful in men's hearts.

Alongside these theories it is possible to venture a third interpretation that focuses on Theseus' power in itself, on his perfection that was as invulnerable as the innocence attributed to him by the first theory, and which Procrustes was incapable of fighting, no matter how many weapons he possessed, and even if the bed existed in its most horrible form. In this case, even if he hadn't fitted the bed, he would have had the power to impose his right through sheer intimidation, ignoring any term or agreement made, not caring whether the result would be against him and forcing Procrustes to accept his point of view even if it was unfair.

The second argument concerns Procrustes' weakness in itself, independent from the existence of Theseus, his own desire, as I pointed out in the beginning for a Theseus to exist, a desire that at the time the hero appeared had overcome Procrustes to such a degree that he would have treated anyone who came along the same way, in spite of the bed, in spite of his devotion to the absolute. In other words, Procrustes was now mature enough to compromise and Theseus was no more than the pretext he needed in order to give in, in a way, consciously fooling himself. If we accept this view, then Theseus was of no significance other than that he came along at the right time, guided by superior powers. Even if this were true it did not, in my opinion, take away from his value. For there are not many people who know how to choose the right time to start something.

The third argument is the limitless plasticity of Theseus, who was able, like clay, to take on any shape Procrustes or his bed desired. The fourth is the cunning persistence of Procrustes who constantly shifted his ideal to suit himself, being true only to the new absolute he kept setting for himself.

Hence the struggle.

And now the problem can be presented with mathematical accuracy.

Let us suppose that neither Theseus nor Procrustes were invulnerable, yet equal in strength, so that the outcome of their conflict is to this day unknown, despite the contrary solutions people, perhaps due to some weakness, like to adopt. If we accept this, then from the very beginning Theseus disputed Procrustes' right to judge and control others so peremptorily.

On the other hand Procrustes posed the question of the existence of the infamous bed, the tradition of its omnipotence and infallibility. Theseus responded by challenging Procrustes on his own ground: Why didn't he put himself to the test on the bed? By what right did he challenge Theseus, when he did not know whether he himself fit the criteria he had set? And so it was that within this purely dialectic contest they went on arguing through the night until daybreak, both sleepless and exhausted, lying in wait for the other to weaken and fall asleep on the fatal bed that would be his end. Because nobody in his right mind would expose himself to the danger of the unknown, even if he had only a thousandth part of a doubt about what the outcome would be.

And this could have gone on for days, for months, for years, with no way out.

That Procrustes was fooled because of his old age and his blurry vision, that he attributed to Theseus a perfection he did not possess, that he was fooled, that he wanted to be fooled — all this was poor consolation for the horrible reality of his defeat.

That he had made with his own hands the weapons that his adversary would use to destroy him is undeniable and tragic. That Theseus won a Pyrrhic victory and that this victory was not due to any superiority but to the generosity of his adversary may also be true. But what good is that, when Theseus has become the omnipotent master of the world and there is no one left to go against him and stand a chance, despite his corrupt sovereignty? As for the bed . . . if there ever *was* a bed, don't we all sleep on it every night?

Hermes and Hermione

The battle over the telephone had subsided around midnight. The men sat down for a snack and Pericles started playing nostalgic *hasapika* and *rembetika* songs from Piraeus on his bouzouki. Then came the time for a smoke. Passing around the big conical cigarettes, dragging on them with their mouths and blowing out through their noses, with eyes languidly half-closed, they sank, and from Volos and Paralos would come Hermes and Hermione, the fleet's rescue boats, to take them all back to the islands, their beds strewn with blossoms, white, red, yellow and light blue hyacinths, their lovely bodies veritable roses, naked and sunburnt, unfolding harmoniously upon the sheets, their eyes becoming sweet and drowsy while all over the sea spread a deathly calm.

The ships' steam whistles belong now to memories.

It was time now for the moon to rise, like a red orange from behind the Trikorfa mountains. In the distance, Hydra. Tomorrow the weather will change. A north wind or a nor'easter, whispered Miaoulis. Tomorrow we'll round the cape. And then hoist sail for the open seas. Those were his words. And from Hydra will rise to the sky the sacred smoke until the day of the great storm, when the torrents and squalls obliterate all these things, these flowers, these funnels, these iron hulls, these illusions, until the water takes its revenge over steel, because in the end water always wins over steel and man, and eats away continuously at the land, licking and biting it, undermining it, until the time comes for it to crash forever to the bottom of the sea, this virgin Greece of ours.

Penthesileia

Passing through the vast countryside I noticed many lights, and groups gathered on the terraces, and the large windows opened and the ladies leaned out taking a little air, ladies made of all kinds of green metals, ribbons, and crystals. The fever had pierced the metal and had penetrated the softer innermost layers of moisture and sorrow, where the seat of all pain resides, where all the poisons collect and empty drop by drop from peoples' hearts. Many describe this unimaginable process in the liveliest colors. We all have somewhere inside us, hidden or unexpressed, some memories from this strange land. Just as the paths of life curl up and disappear in the thickest forests, in stationary dreams, so does this almost symbolic sorrow sometimes stay a little on your lips, in your eyes, and on your lovely hair, O Penthesileia. A small part of all our life, your life passes like a ship that leaves port and disappears into the blue.

Who We Are

We live in a state of complete clairvoyance if I can judge from the few examples I have — we communicate across immense empty distances that would frighten any explorer. We arrive precisely at the same conclusion without calculation — without any planned trajectory. We are mathematically identical and psychically equivalent to a mysterious missile that cannot be placed in the usual category of giant earthly projectiles. We have been running on parallel lines since birth — every time one exists the other exists too — the devil or the angel. Every time Pleasure shows up we greet her as a beautiful stranger. A lady passing through our city, whom we spontaneously honor with displays of arms, quick glances, visits, and hand-kissing in enclosed automobiles — for she is, after all, a courtesan. All our thoughts gather at a single point in the universe, and from that point — which you may easily guess — with no delay, no tears, no perfumes, everything begins. In a coffeehouse we frequent, they know us by a Persian name. They know us as Dariul or Siriul, names such as these. As for Sachnaz, the princess of fairy tales, we see her whenever we imagine her, in the intoxicating fumes of opium. The religion of the old fire worshippers has been replaced with some promises of pilaf in the next world. But who — apart from the gullible, ever believed in such things? Unfortunately it's all taken for granted since we're going to die someday, and in the final reckoning the madman is right. Shouldn't someone put mankind outside the pale — voluntarily — for a whole generation? Shouldn't we stop having children? — since it's clear we're having them to be devoured by the secret Moloch we're openly preparing in the undergound factories (the bombs of Jules Verne would pale before them). "Bombs, then, gentlemen, or children — otherwise we'll go on a permanent sexual strike." The speaker is a blonde and she's recommending the sterilization of infants when they are born. And we've advanced even further than that. It's time for us to withdraw altogether. An earth that would be a peaceful desert full of tombs would be better than an earth covered from one end to the other with frightful scorching wounds. And when the mysterious aliens come from other worlds, they would puzzle and wonder why our civilization disappeared for no apparent reason. Wouldn't it be better for the grain to grow wild as the next-to-last person wanders about in the vast emptiness with a vague memory crossing his brain? In this and in no other way should we end — *Sic transit Gloria Mundi.*

A Classical Education

All my life I thought Homer was blind. Now I think he existed. Later I might change my point of view and adopt the current theory. Has anyone any idea what is now the most current of current theories? When I was a child I thought Homer was a hostage. Since I had not been forced to learn any lines of Homer by heart, I can now recite a few. And there's no shortage of them.

Mēnin aeide thea Pēleiadeo Achillēos . . .
Andra moi ennepe Mousa polytropon hos mala polla planchthēe epei Troiēs . . .

I was lent a book of Homer's verse by my nurse. She, although illiterate, was a classical scholar. She nursed me on Homer and other stories. But I rejected these beverages when I came of age — around the age of reason — and I turned to other younger breast-feeding females. One after another they all turned out to be male-oriented. I had no other choice than do the same. My history teacher had no other milk to give me except his words. My teacher of language taught me how to punctuate imaginary sentences without words. The teachings of History and the teaching of Literature I got with my mother's milk. My mother's name was Hellas. She was young and beautiful. Still young and beautiful, she brought me forth on a platter and offered me to her husband Eros who tried to devour me. But I gave him small change in manuscripts to eat instead. He still asks me for more and that's why I keep on producing. To write is an

occupation, says Terence, or was it Ovid? Not to write is restful
if moderately indulged in. I forgot who said that. Yet some have
misconstrued it as idleness. I was barely fifteen when I was
introduced to Demosthenes. I found him very nice. Although the
story about the pebbles with which he filled his mouth was true,
I believed in it. After all Rimbaud by the age of fifteen had already
written "The Drunken Boat." I wonder sometimes if I hadn't
missed the boat then by being occupied with catching fish
instead. I had a bearded uncle called Demosthenes, a great uncle
called Xenophon and a plain uncle called Aristotle. With so many
classical names in my family how could I ever go wrong. I didn't
lack examples, yet I didn't profit by them. I only heard about
rhetoric much later, from the waiters in the cafés who knew all
the tropes in the trade. I will never forget their discourses on the
tragedy of Government. I also found the prostitutes very eloquent.
One of them, an attractive redhead used to call me her golden
boy. The prostitutes reminded me a lot of the ancient Greeks.
They didn't care much about their bodies. They preferred the
money. Then I discovered the nuns, who cared more about their
souls than their reputations. I've often wondered why God needed
such a large harem of spiritual wives. He must be no different
from Oriental potentates, wanting them all to himself and virginal
too if possible. In my maiden speech on graduation day I
committed many an anacoluthon, not out of ignorance but
because of my youth. Even though I was inexperienced I didn't
consider them as errors but as components of speech. I was
never more applauded than when I hadn't said much. The
brighter the light the greater the darkness. Wisdom and
Ignorance aren't crazy about each other. Yet they met secretly in
many places once upon a time. What a pity they don't do it any
more.

When a poet encounters another poet he must take off his hat
and bow politely, with an ironical smile toward his colleague. He
must do the same when he encounters sensibility. I was once
offended by such behavior. But now I've become used to it. One

of my earliest adolescent loves was called Eva. How could she? All these were just stories but they were authentic. As a token of love I kept on falling and hurting my knee. Patroclus I was told had died in a chariot crash from tetanus. Was Homer so totally ignorant of the causes of his hero's death, or was he only pretending? He is now mainly remembered for exactly that. You can always claim naiveté when you have nothing else to declare. My first reading of Homer was in Greek. Only later did I read him in Spanish. Many dirty schoolboy jokes circulated in Homeric garb. I blush to think of them now. Untranslatable puns:

Cale psoli dans un mouni. . .

Hemos d'erigeneia ephane colodachtylos Eos . . .

Piling insult on injury someone changed the name Eos to Manto, in order to also revile the daughter of Tiresias. What a bunch of disrespectful barbarians schoolboys can be. However from this revolt the Promethean view of the world was born. It's like killing one stone with two birds. I now realize that I too like everyone else read Homer in vain. He taught me nothing. Plato was right. Poets are too immoral to be of any use for education. A moralist who ceases to be a poet becomes a philosopher. Yet Plato was very intolerant of philosophers. He took great pains to refute them. He even confessed his unbounded admiration for Homer in order to better condemn him. Nothing is more delicious than condemning what you most admire. Though he admired Socrates even more than Homer he let others condemn him. Because of this act of courage he has been accused ever since of having had too much passion. My classical education was finally completed by World War II. Hitler's barking shed ample light on the mania of orators for forms of speech and legalistic solutions. For Hitler defended all his transgressions of International Law with meticulous arguments that were flawless. Like Plato, he even hated degenerate art. And evil books of literature. He was a classical hero. Achilles could not have done better, or worse. My reaction was to write very effeminate and decadent verses which drew thunder and lightning from the Colossus of Maroussi, my first editor. "Bunch of queers the whole

13

lot of you poetasters, sluts, babblers. What we need is a real man an epic poet. Another Homer." Although I was only eighteen when he published my effeminate verses, he was right about me. I was in love with the only person I hadn't met. His name was Death. I wanted to make love with Death. Perhaps my dead father? Death obliged and paid me a visit in the guise of the German army. I had to wade over corpses to attend University. But these cartloads of dead were not the classical dead . . . the dying warriors of undying beauty. They were mediaeval deaths as in Bosch and Dürer. I died many comfortable deaths at that time, thus completing my sentimental education in a Gothic environment, which disappointing as it was, introduced me to romanticism, and so onwards to surrealism. From the Greeks I learned how to write in balanced sentences, especially from those authors whose sense of symmetry earned them a reputation far beyond their merits. And here the comparison ends; although it was long-winded it was not too Homeric. Now I'm a lover of nothing more than everything when it is something. In other words my classical education although ended has continued to be no less fruitful than before.

A New Poetic Movement

Suddenly a new poetic movement manifested itself out of the blue. It consisted of a number of poets, about fifteen, who all appeared dressed in the same clothes in public and recited lines of poetry that belonged indifferently to one another. In fact they called themselves the INTERTEXTUALS and they recited continuously in waves, each a sentence, until the fifteenth had done his bit. They claimed in fact to be one person in spite of being many. So they banned, provisionally, the use of *I*, and referred to themselves as *they*. They did not use the royal *we* either, for it had been abused by the poets of the thirties who surmised they spoke also for someone else and not just themselves. This presumption was obnoxious to *them*, because they only spoke for themselves and a select group of others, who were also and always *them*. These *them* then, founded a kind of transcontinental current which went back and forth at the same speed from coast to coast. From them to them it was just a matter of seconds. Communications thus speeded up became a constant "in contact" situation. The collective self formed by the INTERTEXTUALS was later refined by face surgery and height-lifts which made them all look identical. They also underwent voice operations so that the same voice issued from a number of only ostensibly different throats. However, the signals were sometimes contaminated and the wrong ones issued. This involved numerous cancellations of previous invitations. The main poetic work consisted of T-shirts and trousers, all the same grey colour. On them was imprinted their logo, I-TEXTS. Some people mistook these for an ad for textiles, and went to the readings, expecting a shop where they could buy clothing. Cruelly disappointed, they ended up not buying anything they heard. In the end the INTERTEXTUALS decided that there should be no different sexes among them so they all had themselves neutered and castrated and sewn up. In this manner they preserved the purity of their caste plagued by the obsession of difference. I must however grant them a great innovation: the desire, manifested for the first time in this century, not to be original. This in itself constituted an enormous advance in poetic mentality over other schools or styles, whose originality had lapsed from overuse and abuse. To inherit passively a lack of originality is very different from proclaiming it as a virtue. In this, their great shibboleth, they became unsurpassable. And after many generations they managed to rewrite verbatim quite spontaneously and intentionally the *Iliad* and the *Odyssey*, without looking at the text. For this feat alone they will be remembered forever, in the long twilight of poetry that followed. For after that no one ever dared write another line that was not copied from the *original feat* — in other words, their identical word for word spontaneous copy of the *Iliad* and the *Odyssey*.

Helen of Troy

In reality Helen of Troy's name was Helen of Ploy. Not Play as some think. She was too stiff to be toyed with. She was, if it is permitted to say it, an idol. A matinee idol. Marilyn Monroe claimed her and came close to impersonating the fickle Goddess. But she was left behind by playwriting. Sad story, she hanged herself from a tree in Rhodes. Did she deserve it? Her brothers recovered the statue when Theseus stole it. No fool Euripides when he claimed that's what Paris took. He took it to Rome with him but it was too soon for the British Empire to be born. Lord Chesterfield did that for him later. He invented the cigarette. Do we have to, by all means, define it in a sentence? Discuss Coleridge's use of repetition in the mire of the Ancient Mariner. Not a single word of the speech was ever opened later than five o'clock, closing time. Thunder or Light, bellowed the priest coming out of the cave. Half of them said Yes, while the other half chose Thunder. Both were very blunt until they grew up to become even tougher. Imitative magic? Yes by all means. Not by only a few. You rascal, you know all the answers. Except one. What was that? Are the heroes of Homer plain and simple homespun country folk ploughing the rivers of their underworlds with their delirious imagination? Yes. And the rain of fertility and the powercuts caused by lightning made pigs out of us all. Birds of prey meant to revive the forces of nature, sleeping their beauty sleep. Heroines of a single furrow. Heroes of the central frown on the brow. God's fertilizers, collective chemicals. Do battles imply all the people or only some of the people? Anything cut in two would still be an Epic even if it were only a worm! Have you decided which? Don't laugh, please, it'll make the others angry. By which I meant Paradise may be lost again, next time around.

What Do You Make
of the Problem of Sex?

Personally the problem of sex, which I know does exist, doesn't bother me at all. I've never given it a second thought. Only a first one. And that, as briefly as possible. I'm convinced that all those books on sex talk about nothing at all. They love inventing problems so that people can feel involved. Involved in what? But in sex of course. What an illusion. It's the same with pornographic books and movies and other stunts of this kind. Real acts, nude theater. At its best sex is theater. When it's on stage it is as convincing as the actors make it. But behind the scenes in dark bedrooms, it's a myth. I grant you this myth has found great exponents in Doctor Jung, Freud and Havelock Ellis. But even they have to connect it either with fairy tales or fantasies to make it convincing. Frank Harris, for instance, did his best to propagate gossip about himself and women. He was wrong. History has never forgiven him this literal approach. Not that it was scandalous, far from it, but because it was not acceptable to write down as real what had been imagined. As for the New Sexology or Sexual Therapy, as they call it, that all started with Reich, who went to prison for it. He invented the orgasm, another myth. It is well known now after much research that the orgasm doesn't exist. How could such a thing exist? I ask you. . . .It's really preposterous. Ask any man, any woman, put them on a stand with a jury and an audience to describe this. . .event. You will see they will soon begin to stumble on their words, they will blush, they'll say er, well, hum, you see. They will exhibit everything that

19

has been classified as symptoms of lying. If you wish you can bring a lie detector to the rescue. It will record high tension such as only people lying exhibit. So then how can you take anything in that realm seriously? I ask you? Does sex exist? But what about arousal? What about it? That's just a little birdie about to take off. Remember the ancients often depicted it with wings. So there. The Victorians were absolutely right in representing their heroes and their heroines as totally sexless. It was not a sinister attempt to hide what's underneath. On the contrary, it's an attempt to be candid, open, to tell the truth. But often, when confronted with the truth, people mistake it for a lie. It's happened all along. And it's happening once more.

How I Met Ionesco

I met Ionesco exactly fifty-two times next July the fifth. The first time I met him was in a train crossing the channel to England. He was in the same compartment, with his wife and daughter. All three were reading a book from which now and then I captured a sentence flying in the air. A large fish appeared in the window and was peering at us with glazed eyes. An eagle walked in from the corridor and settled on my shoulder. A boa constrictor slithered down from the Alarm Signal. And a lot of jungle creepers started to grow around us until we were completely separated by the intervening jungle. The next time we met was on another train going to Stuttgart, Germany, where a play of his was being performed. Again his wife and his daughter were with him and we shared the same compartment. This time it was a sleeper. Ionesco brought out a violin and played for two hours. I went to sleep and dreamt that Einstein was teaching me the violin. Then I met again with Ionesco in a train returning to Paris from Milan. He seemed very agitated. He was worried about the customs officers. I asked him if he was gun-running as usual. He grew very pale and stuttered a reply I didn't catch. Then came the time when we met on the train going to Amsterdam. Once more he had been invited to attend the opening of a play. He told me that soon he would become a member of the Academy and that then he would have his own private train and private station since the Academy, as it was well known, provided all its members with free transportation anywhere in the world. The

Academy itself was situated, according to Ionesco, in a Grand Terminal not used by the public, in the very heart of Paris. Next time Ionesco and I met was on an express going through Catalonia. There was a crash and Ionesco and I died. But we were resurrected in the next chapter for the purpose of the plot. The author of the book had not finished his novel yet. The last time Ionesco and I met was on the Orient Express steaming out of Istanbul. Ah, that was the greatest meeting of all. We couldn't stop laughing, we laughed throughout the whole journey. Each time we looked at each other we laughed until hours later both of us exhausted by so much laughing had dinner in the *Wagon Restaurant*. The joke was about how I had told him that I had met Ionesco fifty-two times already and it was always on some train or other and each time I mentioned a train, for example the Krackow-Moscow Thursday passenger-and-goods train, or the Transiberian, or the Shanghai Express or the train from Olympia to Salonika, we would break into peals of laughter, for he thought that I didn't know he was Ionesco and that I was making it all up.

Simoon

A vigilant eye flashes over the land like a searchlight. It sweeps across the continents in search of a sign. A sign that something significant is happening, somewhere. Gliding over a dead donkey it illuminates a hole into which I am whispering my last secrets. Somehow the beam of ghostly light strays gently over my hand, writing these lines. It stops, astonished for a second, and reflects itself. It has found and recognized the event. Someone has at last understood it. Someone is writing about writing about writing. The beam has pierced through the night of criticism and obtained access to a brain. A tawny odd looking brain resembling a lion's mane. A brain resembling the lion itself. The brain yawns. A huge black hole opens and the beam is engulfed. Helplessly it flows inside, trapped in an area from which there is no escape. I am now able to follow the life of the beam, to compute its path as it rapidly disintegrates, swallowed by the total throat into which it has returned. The throat of my awareness as a separate being. Somewhere an academic symposium is being held where words are eaten from plastic dishes with metal pincers. Words are being stripped of their lobster-like carapaces. Their tender hard-boiled insides are delicately chewed by rapacious teeth flashing in the dimly lit hall. As the light dies, the scene shifts. We are now in the desert. El Kafr is sitting in his tent while the *simoon* is raging. Quietly he sits smoking his long pipe of hashish. The gardens of the Magreb are blooming. The trees heavily laden with flowers perfume the Mediterranean night. Stealthy silent assassins drift out of doorless entrances and float down the road on a wicked ray of moonlight. They have been paid to kill the lover's husband. They have been paid to abduct the mustachioed bride. They have been asked to spare the little child. Yet they spare no one. Cruel daggers flash in the moon's light and the beam like a foaming waterfall is engulfed by the brain close to the weir. How weirdly and casually it flows out. In the old rusty taps the water foams like soap. The cervix is invaded. Nerves are jangling loosely in the wind. Sea-moon. *Simoon.* The flaps of El Kafr's tent are fluttering gently. Sea-moon. *Simoon.* You are let out of the stable. A handsome young filly. A girl. A boy. In the bloom of adolescent light. Your cervix is invaded by left handed monsters. She is dead. Her plastic doll observes certain mechanical movements. Feeds the children. Tucks them in bed. Speaks to them from a tape incorporated in her perfect semblance. The mechanical mother performs little tasks. She is there. Goes to bed. Gets up in the morning. Cooks the meals. Sits at table. Says a good-will prayer. Drives them to school. She is there in the kitchen washing dishes. In the studio painting pictures. Marvellous automatic paintings emerge. Nonbiodegradable wind shimmers behind plastic curtains. Artificial flowers grow on the beaches. The deserted beaches of the imagination filled with embryonic beauty near the restless biodegradable sea. Words are being charged into young brains. A comic-strip movie is playing in the sky. In vain I try to assemble the facts. El Kafr nods his head. The gagged prisoners are dragged in. They are stripped. El Kafr cherishes every piece of their clothing. He encloses them in an iron box. Then the prisoners are ordered to plug into each other. Death watched the scene, sharpening her scimitar smile. Death you old Turk you haven't quit this task of dissolving El Kafr's hashish dreams into nothingness. The assassins wait for the old man to arrive. When he arrives it will be on a dead donkey. The resurrected donkey worshipped by the mindless people on the plains. A vigilant eye spreads over the land like a prison yard searchlight. I have mastered the past and the present. The garden of delight is laden with dead fruit. A red poppy grows from the eye socket of a corpse. Every now and then the mongols descend through the clouds and blur the windows with fighting. The light needs revitalizing. Midnight strikes on an empty tank. The oil explodes in phosphorescent letters. My fingers try to catch the wind. *Simoon.* El Kafr, the naked prisoners. Everything fades and disappears. . . . A powerful ray of artificial light is trying to fill up a gaping black hole, a yawning abyss. . . . The abyss of my brain.

The Jaguars

for C.P. Kavafis

The Jaguars are coming. Yes. They are coming, closing in on
all sides. It is high time for the Jaguars to arrive. They are all
coming tomorrow. Very early in the morning before breakfast.
Not just a few but many. Perhaps even thousands if not in the
hundreds of thousands. They are coming for sure. That's what
they said when they said they were coming. Tomorrow at three
o'clock, to be more precise. The Jaguars. Many of them unspotted.
Others just striped or black. Grey and pink Jaguars are unlikely
to come. All kinds, all sizes, all shapes. Green yellowish eyes
flashing in the night. Those who say they're not coming are fools.
All the more fools are they, since they don't know what they're
talking about. They have been sighted already not so far away
from the town. I mean the city, the walled city. For we are still
unattached to any form of civilization that's not ours. The
everlasting bones chewed to death. Not a single letter still alive
to tell the tale. The Jaguars although somnolent are hungry for
letters. And for music too beneath those stubborn skulls. It's been
said they were overcome once by music. But that's long ago and
now they don't appreciate music any more. The telegrams have
all stated it clearly.

They are arriving in great numbers over rivers and forests,
over steppes and tundras, over deserts and uninhabited areas.
They are all converging here. What are they seeking? What
reeking rotten flesh are they after? Some people say it's all right
to give them parchments to eat. Others say they only demand

salads, or honors. Only a few suspect the truth. The Jaguars have to be fed with babies' flesh. No other will do. Is the sky electrical with semantic leaps? Is a man enamelled with memories unable to live long enough to see all his expectations fulfilled? The snarled events of his life will form quite a long list of retributions. But enough philosophizing. Will this man ever be? Since I wrote this the Jaguars have surrounded the city. They are trying to scale the walls with yelps and cries and growls. This is not going to be easy for them. Their leader Edward Jaguar is ready to parley. They demand a hostage. Contemplating the sea of Jaguars, some of us are beginning to have misgivings. What do they really want? As I was standing there looking from the highest pyramid of our town, it suddenly dawned on me. My ancestors, the priests, would have done nothing less than what I'm about to do. I now understand what all these Jaguars are about. This is going to be as difficult to describe as a Werner Herzog film. But I must do it to the end. The townspeople are imploring me to do it. A great calm has descended on the hoards of Jaguars as before a storm. The air is filled with electricity. The townsfolk are begging me on their knees. Then suddenly, in a flash of lightning which illuminates the skies with thunderous claps from clouds of dust and steam, it occurs to me what the Jaguars are really after. Why they have come such a long way over oceans and deserts. They want me. And more specifically my penis, or rather my phallus, if you wish. Why hadn't I thought of that before? We humans are so blind to other animal's desires. Yes, my phallus of obsidian, symbol of power over generations of priest-kings, I repeat it without shame. I'm the object of their hunger. The decision was taken in an instant. From my neighbor the butcher I borrowed his elegantly carved electrical saw, bearing the head of a Jaguar. Pardon me, Depardieu, for plagiarizing you, I muttered and I severed it with one quivering thrust and threw it to them. A great roar rose as they leaped up to catch it. The one who caught it was immediately devoured by the others, who devoured those who had devoured him, until in a carnage of mutual devoration not a single Jaguar was left. But no, I am mistaken, one was left.

It was Edward Jaguar who had consumed them all. Together we contemplated the rising sun, the beast and myself. The sun rose over the field of the most majestic carnage in the history of the world. And as the odor of blood and flesh subsided, I looked at myself in the mirror that Edward Jaguar was holding up to me with his teeth. I was transforming into a woman. Breasts had grown where only tits had been, my long hair became shinier and curlier and black as ebony. My eyes sparkled, while the gathering crowds applauded wildly, not their savior, but their savioress, not their hero but their heroine: Myself. Rejuvenated from an old man to a young woman. While Edward Jaguar himself, already half-man, was holding my hand with carnivorous glee.

Beauty and the Beast

Edward Jaguar never became totally human. His animal self was still evident even after his animalectomy. The head remained Jaguar-like. He spoke, but then he had always been able to speak. His body, although he walked upright, was more Jaguar-like than human. His teeth and claws remained especially formidable. Sleeping with him was much closer to an act of bestiality. Even as a man I had never indulged in it. But now as a woman it was really strange to me. I have heard rumors of women making love with their animals. I had never really given it much thought. But now when confronted with these teeth, these claws that could spring at me any moment, I realized that the thrill of love could be mingled with the fear of death. This description is becoming too intimate for my taste. . . . Yet I cannot resist the details. That shiny black skin. That extraordinary tenderness and love of the animal. The feeding times when he will only take the raw flesh from my bare hands as delicately as a little pussycat. The purring. The growling whimpers when he makes love, to me. Our long walks in the outskirts of the jungle, and of course my fears that jealous humans will kill him. My jealousy in case he finds a female Jaguar and runs away. How I would risk my life in the jungle looking for him. How I would wait for him faithfully to come back. How when he is angry with me he climbs trees and refuses to come down or take food for days. How I have sometimes locked him out of my room and he remains all night outside my door whimpering. This description is becoming too intimate for my taste. Yet I cannot resist indulging in it. I know I take risks and people may think dreadful things of me after they read this. But I have to be faithful to what I believe and honest with myself. Although honesty in the general sense is only a bourgeois value, a safeguard for merchants, a business ethic, yet honesty to oneself is the writer's prerogative. It is even an obligation, a duty, a pleasure. The thought has crossed my mind. A desire so terrible and obscure that I dread to utter it. I now have only one obsession left in my life. I want to become an animal. I want to be able to run freely with my beloved Edward, to climb trees without fear of falling. To hunt with him and eat raw flesh. Does that sound as terrible as all that? Have I not got the right to belong to any species I like? No question about it. When we went to the Jaguar-priest and asked him to perform the transformation, it was like getting married in the Church. We both stood before him and he asked me: "Will you take Edward to be your lawful wedded animal?" Blushing, I said "Yes," with all the passion I could work up in my voice. He too growled his assent when the priest said, "Will you take Nan O to be your lawful wedded wife?" And we held paws, and kissed, with scrapy tongues. "All right," said the priest, "now run along, my children, and have fun. . . ." And we ran off, I for the first time on all fours and smelling the odors of the forest, a real symphony of smells, as my nose became sensitive to them, and pricking up my ears at the slightest sound . . .

The Other Side of the Story

(A tribute to Claude Levi-Strauss)

The Jaguars, on the other hand, have given a completely different account of this story, distorting the facts. According to the *Forest Jaguar Annals*, I was a traitor to my people and negotiated a peace with *Edward Jaguar* — at the price of cutting off my penis. Once my penis was cut, I was at his mercy — because he ate it and acquired my magical powers. They then proceeded to give a shameful account of how Edward Jaguar took me around with him — passing a collar over my neck and holding me on a leash. The price of my humiliation had saved my people, they claim, who were allowed to evacuate Jaguar City, which was then infested with Jaguars. Yet, from my earliest childhood, I had heard from the mouths of the Jaguar Priests exactly the opposite version. There had been, they said, a Jaguar Princess who fell in love with my ancestor Nan-O. She visited him secretly every night in his tent inside the pallisade of the tribe's forest habitation. From there she returned to the walled city and had a child by him — a human — who had a man's body, but a Jaguar head. This monster, when he grew up, ravaged the neighborhood of the walled city until all the Jaguar tribes of humans decided to join an all-out assault. The walled city was taken, and the Jaguars within were caught by surprise. They had been feasting at one of the innumerable festivals. The humans then chased the animals to the forest and took over the walled city, which they named in their language, Jaguar City. After many centuries, the Jaguars decided to ask for help, and convoked all their species —

leopards, cougars, panthers, mountain lions, cheetas, tigers; all except the lion, adding even such wild cats as the lynx — and made a general assault on the city. It was at that point that I intervened, and through the strategem of the cut penis, *vanquished them*. Now Edward Jaguar was not the only remaining Jaguar. There were still some left hidden in the forest. But since then they never ventured out. However, they told their offspring this distorted version of my feat, and ordeal, presenting me as the vanquished victim. This version seemed to please their thick, stubborn heads. Since Edward and I had been married, they could indulge freely in a little fantasizing about the whole relationship between me and him, especially since we hunted the same prey as *they* did, and that made them very angry.

a terrace is a man's only love

For my Aunt Dory

A man is sitting on his terrace. . .he leans on the terrace like
a woman who leans against a man. . .the man is the child of the
terrace. . . .The terrace when he was a child was like his father
. . .he has always been a child on the terrace looking over
below. . .to associate terraces with moslem countries only is
wrong. . .it is like saying that nights are christian and that days
are pagan. . .these old errors must not be repeated for the sake
of clarity. . .but what is clarity. . . Clarity is precision. . .but
what is precision. . .is it a man standing on a terrace overlooking
the sea. . .what are these grave thoughts that overcome him
when he listens to the humming of the boats. . .the terrace is the
man's nest. . .it is where he roosts. . .the terrace is the man's
branch. . .he sits on it like a bird. . .the terrace is the man's
sea. . .he floats on it. . .he swims in it. . .the terrace crawls on all
fours. . .it is unable to lift its head and look at the man. . .the
terrace is the man's grandmother. . .it is his benefactor. . .it is his
oldest friend. . .the terrace represents all the ages of man. . .the
terrace is a hypothesis to which the man wholeheartedly
subscribes. . .it is the end of reason and the beginning of
serenity. . .the terrace is hot. . .it is deadly in the summer at
noon. . .in the evening the terrace is a real haven. . .the man on
the terrace sits on a chair. . .he looks toward the sea. . .or toward
the mountains or toward the town. . .the man sitting on the
terrace is dead. . .he is silent and motionless like an old log. . .
the man on the terrace breathes in the cool air of the night. . .he

is invisible. . .his thoughts are invisible too. . .he breathes them out and they form patterns on the floor of the terrace. . .the terrace is a lonely horizontal wall. . .the man's expectations are dashed by this wall. . .they are reduced to flat dimensionless shapes. . .the vertical wall's shadow divides the terrace in two halves. . .the man is now standing half-naked on the lit side and half-clothed on the shaded side of the terrace. . .his mind is also equally divided in two. . .like two alternatives that occur to him clothed in light and in shadow. . .they are like two women clothed in white and in black. . .they are sentences spoken once upon a time by the terrace before the man was born. . .now the terrace only reflects the man's inner states. . .his thoughts, his loves, his sadness, his exaltations. . .a ghost crosses the terrace in broad daylight. . .it is a luminous shadow. . .it is the genius of the place. . .it is shrouded and it looks familiar. . .it looks like the column of salt to which it is related by its whiteness and its shape. . . . The man does not see the ghost although it passes right through him. . .the man has his own ghosts to worry about . . .the ghosts of his memory which crowd in his brain. . .the man gets up. . .he walks slowly across the terrace as if he were crossing a desert. . .the desert which he is crossing is that of his own mind. . .he may die of hunger or thirst in the middle of it. . .he may be abandoned by his mind and go mad. . .or he may abandon it for some dark enterprise such as falling in love. . . the magnificence of his despair is represented by the terrace which has now taken immense proportions. . .it seems endless. . .and yet the man's life is strictly circumscribed by its beginning and its end. . .since when has a man stood on the terrace of his heart without knowing it. . .since when has a terrace been the roof of a man's head. . .since when has a terrace been standing inside a man or on him. . .with one sweep of his hand the man brushes the terrace away from his field of thought. . .he is now asleep below the terrace as he had feared he would be. . .someday. . .now the terrace walks over him perpetually and he can do nothing about it. . . .

How I Wrote Some of My Books

for Raymond Roussel

As far as I can remember I began to write — one morning at dawn when I was five years old and my governess was still asleep — with a stolen pen, and I wrote till the sun went down to everyone's astonishment. When the lamps were lit I went on writing deep into the night until the pen fell from my hands in the small hours of the morning. In my sleep I picked up my pen once more, and went on writing in the manner of a somnambulist for the next few weeks, in spite of everything, or even because of it. No admonitions, scoldings or punishments could stop me, and even then my inspiration did not run out. My room was in a sorry state with sentences, paragraphs, chapters, all piling up to the ceiling, while new manuscripts surged up ceaselessly from below running down the stairs to the apartments of our neighbors who had to slash through a jungle of words to get into their kitchens or bathrooms. Soon the town was flooded and the traffic jams were terrific. As they spread beyond the city, my words began to fill up the universe. They stretched in huge luminous sentences so long that even I could not read them from end to end without forgetting how they had begun. A slow drizzle of words began to fall on the world and people looked up into the sky and wondered where it came from. Could it be that God's hand, writing the famous word, had gone crazy? Someone must be writing up there, they said placidly, and shrugged their shoulders. It was then when a flood was just about to submerge the continents that I stopped in the nick of time and gave up personal creation. I decided the effort was too great and that from now on I would only use intermediaries. I developed a system of possessing every available writer telepathically and guiding his or her hand at will. This process became automatic after some practice on my part. And now all the books written by others are in reality by me. This method is far more comfortable than the previous one and has turned me into a universal ghost writer. In my new role I remain strictly anonymous. But I don't mind. It's a pleasure to browse through the book stalls in the terminals and remember each book as I conceived it. I don't need to read them, of course, because I know what's in them. All I have to do is flash the title through my mind and the rest comes back instantly. I now look forward to the third phase, which I am about to call The End of Writing. In this next period I will be able to make direct contact with my readers and dispense with all this mass of hired labor of middle persons who I am currently employing and whom I have playfully referred to as *Hired Hieroglyphs*, upon which promptly someone wrote a book of poems with that title. A totally insignificant Greek poet. It makes me laugh when people refer to him as the author. For every one of my thoughts is picked up immediately, as merchandise in the supermarkets, by those people currently known as creators. My trashy thoughts are picked up by hacks, and my better moments by the most talented. However in the future I will do away with all this clumsy machinery and I will feed my readers directly with the real thing. My raw thoughts. They will then experience something resembling their breast-feeding age, a total bliss, sometimes referred to as an altered state of consciousness, a sort of dream-like state of ecstasy. The end of reading and writing will then occur. The written signs and sounds will be replaced by a permanent matrix of total meaning in which everything will be inserted as part of reality. Trees, stones, mountains, events, numbers, the people themselves, will be *the* language. Everything will read and be read simultaneously, if that word has any meaning left. All will then experience a totality so wonderful, so rich in depth and breadth that it will closely resemble what today we call insanity. As meaning proliferates endlessly communication will break down. No exchange of information will any longer be possible, thank god. Each one will live as plants do, for himself, in himself, and by himself, in a state described by the Jainas as Kayvalyam or total detachment. During this cycle the Universe will disappear with everything that is in it, and I and all the others will go on experiencing absolute selfness — the ultimate — indifferent to what could still possibly be going on around us and forgetful of each other's existence. That will be, no doubt, the final split second which is bound to last for all eternity. Till then let's hope that no one will blow my cover and foil my plans. Keep your fingers crossed.

Anastronomical Details

for A. Jarry

Anastronomy is part of the Science of MUST, whose subject matter is always grey; Aniconomy is another field of this vast domain encompassed only by the complementary limits of the Possible and the Impossible; and whose beauty consists solely in the absolute contiguity of every area of study and its plasticity expressed in terms of being able to replace at a moment's notice any subject by any other and in this manner making it possible for any line of argument to both reciprocate and continue the previous one as if no change had actually occurred in the almost seamless capacity of things to join together without a single crack in the smooth surface of which even the most exercised eye could not discern any artificially collated parts; furthermore, to extend this method of thinking in any given direction simultaneously and almost equidistantly from the original nucleus from which it all started; nothing will interfere as long as all possibilities are kept within an arm's reach and not held to be exclusively in the service of one or the other dogmatically defined cause whose end is not necessarily in view as more and more beginners invade every square inch of its terrain.

We as individuals inserted in a text whose limits are the limits of our life; inside the Cosmic being; handwriter for the multitude of mute matter that speaks through me; my periods and my paragraphs my sentences of nerves and flesh; my dried out parchment skin my ink of blood; the sea rushed into my bedroom; I am blotted into the eternal brain whose archive-holder is my arm; eternally rewritten to the boundaries of the page; in the gravediggers language I am committed to earth; translated into the tomb; the mysterious goat of this oven of totality grazes over me; my third century Roman Buick (Catalogue Vintage) recovered intact from the buried Pompei runs thirty-three miles to a gallon of Poppeas' asses' milk; walls of siren-sounds envelope the ancestral domains; reveal yourself defunct object of words; death on the poet's lap offers him a drink from a baby mushroom's porous skull; typewriter filled with clouds of innocence goes backward in time with a whirring noise; only a pulverized voice screeches through the dead nerve ends; gold, the father, the phallus, and the language: ART (hur RimB) AUDelaire. . . .

Borisofski's Lair

The well of Borisofski — the great empty mouth of the well of Borisofski. The fish in the great empty mouth of the well of Borisofski. The land of the fish of the great empty mouth of the well of Borisofski. The shoulder of the land of the fish in the great empty mouth of the well of Borisofski. The road on the huge shoulder of the fishes' land in the great empty mouth of the well of Borisofski. The man who walks on the road of the huge shoulder of the fishes' land in the great empty mouth of the well of Borisofski. The knout held by the man who walks on the road of the huge shoulder of the fishes' land in the great empty mouth of the well of Borisofski. The handle of the knout held by the man who walks on the road of the huge shoulder of the fishes' land in the great empty mouth of the well of Borisofski. The animal carved on the handle of the knout held by the man who walks on the road of the huge shoulder of the fishes' land in the great empty mouth of the well of Borisofski. The mouth of the animal carved on the handle of the knout held by the man who walks on the road of the huge shoulder of the fishes' land in the great empty mouth of the well of Borisofski. The huge mouth of the animal carved on the handle of the knout held by the man who walks on the road of the huge shoulder of the fishes' land in the great empty mouth of the well of Borisofski. The tongue in the huge mouth of the animal carved on the handle of the knout held by the man who walks on the road of the huge shoulder of the fishes' land in the great empty mouth of the well of Borisofski. The man on the tongue in the huge mouth of the animal carved on the handle of the knout held by the man who walks on the road of the huge shoulder of the fishes' land in the great empty mouth of the well of Borisofski. The knout held by the man on the tongue of the huge mouth of the animal carved on the handle of the knout held by the man who walks on the road of the huge shoulder of the fishes' land in the great empty mouth of Borisofski's well.

Gloomy Reality

Gloomy reality appeared one morning at my door. She was wearing a straw hat with cherries on it, weighed down with memories and filled with fearful threats about the future.

She spoke in a nasal voice and kept her hand in front of her mouth so as not to let me see her missing teeth.

Naturally she was a prude and she didn't accept proposals of marriage or of any other kind. As you must know, she's a literary lady and knows all the ancient texts inside out and backwards, and she knows all the dictionaries by heart. She appeared in a leap year, when no one knew whether they were coming or going.

To the naked eye the Pleiades are a confused group of stars, of a diffuse brilliance, whereas with a telescope, seven bright stars can be seen, those called the Seven Sisters in folklore. Sometimes I ask myself whether human eyes were not once much sharper, and whether they didn't see in the distance, like telescopes, what has now become invisible to ours.

So, *she* was one of the Seven Sisters, the ugliest, and she had remained an old maid without any hope of ever getting a husband. A hermaphrodite woman, a real monster, and almost moustachioed to the point that not too long ago she would have been taken for a soldier in skirts. And she carefully hid her secret lust, and for the eyes of the world she played the *innocent and modest virgin* and the *holy Mary*.

She played a record on the stereo deck. It screeched in an

unbearably broken voice, and the needle scratched it so horribly that my nerves couldn't take it anymore. I covered my face with a pillow so as not to see her, I plugged up my ears so as not to hear her. It was the only way to avoid making love with *gloomy reality*, who had now changed into *naked reality*. That is, into realism — socialist or otherwise, it's all the same. . . . Running into her is always unbearable, whatever the place, whatever the political system she appears in.

Coup D'Etat

Everything was ready. From Syntagma Square to Kou-kouvaounes, all the uniforms stood in line. And everyone who passed by had to sign his name without further ado. Vast expanses, up until then uncultivated, were found this morning covered with red British fabric. Of course the quality was not the same as before the war. But we should not be too demanding. The bridges were never very sturdy. And the Municipal Council had desperately tried for years to overcome the unreasonable resistance of public opinion. Of course there are many versions. One refers to Justinian, the rest compare Greece to a newly felled fir tree. For the moment, let us be content with adding an exclamation mark to the already imposing list and collection of foods bequeathed to us by the Byzantine Empire. At this point I will stress the fact that I never intended to theorize. The nights were very dark. And the pedestrians were in danger of tripping on the nails and falling like Achilles into Hades. But grant me an opportunity to confess adequately. (This word, "adequately," appeared here quite by chance, as I have said before, and indicates a concession to the clergy.)

But I, you, the people, the watchmaker Kasmiris and Prince Makris, are all victims of dark conspiracies and an unprecedented judicial error. And here one could perhaps agree with the famous saying of Kolokotronis: "Sometimes a carnage is necessary, as long as it is in strict keeping with all the rules of calisthenics."

The Way Things Go

We were much too high up here for the voice to be heard below or for the message to reach us from across the bay through the bullhorn. It is true that whatever written notes we sent, they were never answered, and we never saw the postman again nor the paper on which we wrote. Nevertheless there had been no mistake, the plateau could be seen clearly, and the road that led from one wood to the other disappeared as hills became progressively lower by the river, and from there the valley of the reeds spread out, the well-kept gardens all around it, and every night the little town could be seen flooded in light. In the distance lay the sea. Above, the sky, grave and motionless. They say that up here the air is clean and rare and the water full of calcium, hard and cold, and the people seem to be in a trance, the way they stand, reminiscent of ancient gods.

Their words are few and they think only of hunting. On other days they may seem different. Perhaps when the sun is setting behind the mountains as if being slaughtered and in the deep valley the shade becomes stronger and spreads out from ridge to ridge. Perhaps the night comes forth from the plane trees and the blackberry bushes, and hurries up the mountain tops. Perhaps it is born over there in the mountains where our friends live. We see them sometimes through the binoculars as they talk and gesticulate like firs on the mountain sides, as they point toward us, without seeing us, of course, without knowing that we are watching them, without ever hearing what we say about them or what we would like to say. (There are no gramophones here, nor wash basins. The bath tubs are wooden and the water remedial for those who drink it.) Perhaps when the mountains turn red and housewives draw the curtains in their homes, they too want to avoid a meeting that can only be painful. Perhaps they who whisper in taverns are right, and the things they whisper true. Perhaps it was untimely and harmful for letters to be mailed. Perhaps that was why mailmen so often disappeared or were murdered on the beaches. Perhaps that is why nightingales are no longer heard when the sun is shining and when other waters come forth in the forest to sing.

The Triumph of Decadence

The interior remains unexplored, inhabited by barbarian tribes and hostile cultivators of the fertile soil who turn over their crop to ruthless overseers with dark eyes.

They obey. They do not forget that it's the foreign state, a symbol of the Conquest that deprives them of a third of their production.

But they say nothing. From father to son they have grown used to bowing their heads. Blessed be the earth, the generous earth, and the river, the god of fertility. Let us go and light little candles to the small gods and silver votive lamps at the Great God's sanctuary. Let us give palm oil and perfumes to our lady. You see, she likes to make herself beautiful all year round.

Don't misunderstand us. Our wives only dress up and wear perfume on holidays. Other people don't follow these customs. They have their own. Perhaps the conquered do not have an opinion. In silence they find their age-old fortitude. The narrow strip of civilization on the beach isn't very sturdy. Paralyzed by the apathy of the population, it is in danger of being overwhelmed at any moment by the barbaric stutterings of the nomads that inhabit the interior.

The laws and regulations are purposely made to keep under foot the unassimilated element, which was superior in number but not in the diligent expertise needed to handle the affairs of a civilized state that trades with other great nations and competes with them:

a) In the splendor of their army uniforms.

b) In the size and displacement of their ships.

c) In the grandeur and luxury of their palaces.

d) In the variety of ulterior motives aimed at by a clever and cunning diplomacy, in laying claim to the sovereignty and suzerainty of the many regions that are disputed or coveted by other periodically powerful powers and dynasties and tyrants.

e) In the realm of letters (we come first), in the number of texts we have accumulated. In the number of great poets and commentators we have.

In the mysterious evocations of our religions.

In the variety of ways gods are worshipped.

f) In our knowledge of geography and mathematics (we are vastly superior, and in the charting of the lands we are progressing to the extent allowed by the instruments at our disposal).

All year round our shops are full of fabrics, decorations and jewelry, rare dyes, spices, synthetic wool, perfumes and strange beverages, stimulants, aphrodisiacs, tranquilizers, drugs that bring on the most euphoric dreams and whatever other love potions, body and face creams, medicines to bring back to life aging flesh.

And in the secret art of love, our women are taught to give pleasure, being neither vulgarly provocative nor excessively prudish or frigid in bed. They give themselves with reserved fervor and wise movements, their dark bodies offering and receiving equal pleasure. Elegantly dressed and full of grace they walk the streets, their rich hair well-arranged on their heads and their toned bodies visible through the thin togas, their breasts erect, strong curving lines, the black inviting shadow of their womanhood between the thighs. And meaningful glances that promise a rich sensuality to bodies exposed to naked water, to the tonic effect of the sun, and to the desire of adolescent eyes.

In the assembled city of linear construction and balanced roads, in the official facade of the pier, the peristyles and epistyles, the arches and the triangular shapes of the ceiling, the pure pentagon of true creation, the essence of inner destination in the circular arena of naked souls, and finally, the muffled gurgle of streams in the gardens where artificial birds sing, at the port's glorious semicircle, in the chattering of the sidewalks, the orations at the marketplace, the studied carelessness of the peripatetics, the devotion of students to the dour philosopher, the official study of verbal transformations.

And in the maze of the palace where the courtiers' sneers are heard, the deterioration of respect and trust rules over the young monarch. He is surrounded by naked swords and helmets, he is touched by the erotic gazes of women. He is the center of dark reflexions. He is the most inaccessible. He is the master of vile schemes.

The Windows of Genius

For K.I.V.

The first window was unhappiness. The second window was meaning. The third window was meditation. The fourth window was ingratitude. The fifth window was a definition. The thousand other windows of genius were closed. They didn't open except when you called them by name and their names were unknown and secret, either lost and impossible to find, or half erased and indecipherable.

Once a year, five beautiful cleaning women came and cleaned the five open windows, naked temptresses wearing silk masks that covered their faces and reached down to their breasts. The other windows remained closed and dirty. Dust coated them, frost ate them, rain fell on them, and the wind blew on them through the centuries. They darkened as time passed, and some people said there weren't even windows at all, and that the dim light that remained would go out and the monstrous building of genius itself would be abandoned, empty, and deserted.

Then the reformers came, wanting to name the building, to tidy it up and deliver it to the public. They said it was a mental institution. Disorderly people lived there, so the regular people, the residents, could look after them. And the nameless palace, the great mansion of genius, became unrecognizable and the rascals came and filled it with inarticulate voices, with cries and screams, with raving, with hallucinations, with obsessions, and with many other symptoms they call clinical.

And this new institution worked normally, except that the

50

thousand closed windows of genius wouldn't open, so the rooms couldn't be ventilated according to the wishes of the social reformers, the teachers, the lawyers, the doctors, and the judges. The wind blew through the closed windows. And in the empty rooms there remained the nameless thousand and one names of the unending melancholy of Being.

The Games of the Circle

I light fires to your memory, my secret laboratory because I'm sure you were innocent. They conducted endless evil plots and libels against you. They brought you to me dismembered. I barely managed to put you back together with the solid glue of my will.

But I'm still sure you were innocent. I exhibited you at the window, and the crowds saw you were unharmed after your ordeal. They recognized the miracle. They spontaneously called you a saint. They elevated you to the heavens in spite of the church, the government, and the labor unions.

When I finished you, my work, I no longer had anything to do around here. I left the world and ascended to the heavens where I became a star in the constellation of the Bear, whose hide was nailed upside down.

And I'm still sure you were innocent. I rested my hopes on a new Messiah who turned out to be a fake, and on a worthless invention that simplified the lives of thousands before it proved defective. Since then I have used a golden beam to wash the window where the girl sits and waits for me.

Still certain that you were innocent I made my reckoning and memorized you by rote. After all, the exams were approaching and they would flunk me if I didn't sing to you, Goddess, the wrath, and so forth. When I accepted this assignment I bowed low to you, my vision of the empty land that contained me up until this recent future of a gentleman in a tuxedo with a nail for a head buried in his collar.

And sure as I can be that you were innocent, without false nostalgia, without lawsuits, without knives, I pass you by and leave, never to come back here except to see you again, my old friends, like the fishes in the deep.

The Thieves

All twelve thieves, in modern clothes, welcomed me into the cave. They didn't say anything, but I had the feeling that they all felt the same thing. They were probably thinking it but they didn't say anything, maybe because they had all agreed, maybe because they always hid their feelings, maybe because they didn't want to embarrass me, maybe because they didn't want to speak too bluntly for fear of offending me, or maybe they wanted me to figure it out for myself — that I was the thirteenth thief, the one without a hat, the one they were expecting, the one with whom they wanted to sit down.

The cave was full of candles. Since the days of Noah, I thought, there hasn't been a bunch of more ordinary fellows, never in a hurry, not especially afraid of death, behaving just as if they were all assembled in their own living room, so peaceful, so stylish, so calm that you'd think they were twelve laborers, twelve woodcutters, twelve priests with white beards, twelve fertile hypotheses.

Delicate and polite, they didn't act as though they were about to slaughter me. Every so often they glanced at a timepiece embedded in the rock. "Time is ending," they explained. "It won't last much longer. From now on, we'll live outside time."

"And how will we manage?" I asked uneasily.

"Don't worry, that's why we're here, to take care of it, so it won't be the same old thing."

"That would be horrible," I said.

"Horrible, horrendous. . .we have to face up to it. We'll be in the dark, as though the lights had gone out for a while. Time is ending."

"How can that be?" I asked. "After all, haven't people always said that time is endless? How can it die before we do? I realize that *we* come to an end, but time, isn't time endless?"

"Ssh," they said, "the end is here." They stood silent for a few moments.

Time ended. It died. I heard it gasping in the depths of the cave. Finally they brought it to us. The twelve thieves crossed themselves over the beautiful remains of a young warrior from ancient times. I was the only one who remembered to put two fingers over his eyes and close them. Time had died, but we were still alive. How strange. Think about it: how could we survive if time was gone? "Isn't that unfair?" I asked.

"No, it isn't," the thieves answered. "Time robs, time plunders. Now it's time for it to rest. Now it's our turn."

"Who are you?"

"Who are we?" they answered with dangerous grins. "Do you want to know who *we* are? We're your instincts, your evil instincts that are waking up from their impotent sleep. And the dead time is yourself, along with your ideas, your doubts, and your excessive objections against us. So forward, now, to where we *execute your desires.*

Three Problems of the Sea

For Andreas Embirikos

A

We knew for sure it was an island when we saw the birds. Somewhere near here the sea crashes against the rocks like a woman chained to the land. Somewhere near the shore an ancient pitcher grows cold by an open window, and a potted plant blossoms with absinthe and amaranth. But first we had to cross certain valleys, to hide in dark caves, to carve a smile on the stone, to light on the hills several large fires called for by the needs of castaways and the imagination of poets. When the sea finally appeared it was not as we had always expected it. The shore seemed more deserted, more precipitous, the water tired and dispirited, and further out the sea had grown old. The storm was now raging to the west. Other islands were suffering, other ships in danger. Even though we hurried, it was too late. Our presence on the shore was totally unnecessary. Some wanted to give us at least a formal excuse to be there. But most of us could not hide our concern. We had forsaken the valleys without a pretext. Now, at our feet, the beaches were strewn with debris. Broken pieces of wood, ship accessories, barrels, bottles, cables, and stakes. Every now and then a dead body. Somebody suggested we bury some of them. But right away a new obstacle arose. Were these our people? Or were they foreigners? It was impossible to verify. They were disfigured by the water and the birds had devoured their flesh. By now nobody wanted to go back. Some for fear, some for bitterness, others because they liked to roam the caves, listening to the moaning sea.

B

Totally unexpectedly one night the lighthouse came on. We all knew that the lighthouse was deserted and the light was out. We all thought it was difficult, if not impossible for it to be lit. At once we became suspicious and sent two men to look around. Only one came back, and died in our arms. After that, we didn't dare take further action. The light would come on regularly as soon as the sun was gone, and would go out again at dawn. Nobody dared mention this mystery, let alone investigate it. There was a silent agreement accepted by all, that the subject should not be discussed. Each one on his own was free to think and assume whatever he pleased. But one day I couldn't help it, and as we were eating at the table on the terrace, the whole family together, I leaned over to my grandfather, and without saying a word, pointed to the lighthouse beacon, which had just come on. A look of desperation came over everyone's face. The light started going out; little by little it faded until it was gone and darkness spread all around. After that it never came on again, and everybody, without of course ever saying so openly, considered me responsible.

C

When the sea finally appears, I repeat, nothing can stop us ascertaining that it is real. When the water is agitated by the wind, it turns white and flings itself desperately upon the shores. At night, the sea snores like a person having nightmares. Its smell is unmistakable. The salt on the skin and eyelids, the taste of salt on the lips, the eyes that see ships sailing when we look toward it; those are the signs. They are merely signs, and as long as we live, those are the only kinds of signs we will have of the sea's existence. Perhaps also a few names, Greek or other. And perhaps the testimonies of certain trustworthy people, be they poets or sailors.

Transubstantiation

In the beginning it came and placed itself in the empty market place — a bicycle, and it stood there for a long time. Then the cyclist came and mounted the bicycle, and on the cyclist's shoulder sat a little boy, and inside the little boy's hand there was a ladybug and inside the ladybug was I.

Later on came first a man, a passerby who stood gaping... then he went and another came and wondered...when he had gone a third man came and stood staring like an idiot...and he could not get a thing straight. Then he disappeared and went back to his business. After these then came the wise ones in threes quarreling loudly with each other. And they meant that this can't be and that this is not possible....A trick bicycle standing by itself in the middle of the sea and on the surface of the water without falling. They regarded it as blasphemy that it did not sink because He had walked on the water and the water that came from therein was only a couple of inches deep and not high enough to carry the weight of such a bicycle, with a cyclist mounting and dismounting, with a child on its shoulder and a ladybug in the hand of the kid and with me inside the bug, I the Conniver.

Then the wise men left followed by those who were pedants and who closely examined us. They counted the strokes of the brakes and tested the tires of the chain and tried the strength and the bow of the chain.

They weighed our clothes, gave us food and dissected our

excrements. The result: Zero. Because neither are feelings sufficient in an act of balance nor are arguments enough when we are placed before protocol.

The quarrelsome left us and then came those who were definitely out of it, the strangers and the neutrals.

And they threw coins at us so that the bucket was filled up to the brim, three rounds of their coins, and then the cyclist stepped down, and the little boy climbed down from his shoulders, and he opened his hand and the ladybug, an insect, flew away and then we left too, the cyclist the bicycle and I, and the square was empty as it had been before and afterwards and as it will always be. Forever.

The Black Sun

For Eleni

We come to the conclusion that the sun is black precisely because it is so white. But there is always another way. If you stare at it, it begins to look like a black diamond, revealing the darkness of which it is made. At first there is very little. A line across its bright face like a wrinkle. But it keeps getting stronger, one minute like a dark circle of hair surrounding it, the next like a wreath tightened around its head. Little by little the black rays increase and we begin to feel the difference as we stare into each other's eyes at noon, as if a funeral had suddenly passed between us.

The hand we are holding in ours is released from the things we were used to, and shines inexplicably with a bereavement of its own. The door opens and the wind comes in, in the shape and the voice of a person, the mountains written on its back. What color is the wind that blows from the sea? What weight has a smile when it lights up your face? So then everything is made from the same silk that we once saw turning black by the window, and the shutters can no longer protect anyone from the new evil that disfigures faces, as if a broken mirror were always set up before them. How do our eyes work in lightning? Our skin in fire? What is this shiver when we hear a change in the soul approaching? The sun, like your body, is also a well. Its water is inexhaustible and black as death. Just as the wave on the shore never becomes a flower.

The Hunchback of Notre Dame

I can see for almost thirty miles around. Some call me the human telescope others the inhuman microscope. Walls have no secrets for me. Shutters and windows act as lenses. The trees convey my meaning far and wide. My gift of seeing is not at all limited to just penetrating material structures such as human flesh. Skeletons are my favorite sport. Were it not for my ability to also see deeply in the deadly human soul my life would be much happier. I see hearts and minds clouded by wasted thoughts and emotions. I see reason trampled under by indifference. I see love in a mortal embrace with reason. They both eventually succumb. I see stamp collections from which stands out the *Amanita muscaria* resembling a foggy dawn in a great city. I see light where others only see darkness and desolation. I see the flamboyant poetry of psychotics rising from the mouth of plain neurotics. What less than a guitar can awaken the frenzy of common metals? I ask you, is this the most unreasonable thing to expect from anyone who can breathe?

The Train

In the great crush of the Athens-Piraeus subway, a woman pressed hard onto me from behind.

She whispered in my ear: "You want to trade identities? You'll be me and I'll be you." I turned, with great difficulty, in the crush and I saw a frightful old hag with rotten teeth, like a monkey.

"We're so much alike," she said, and she opened her mouth half a yard wide. I saw that her mouth was the entrance of the subway and on the two walls, I glimpsed electric cables and electric lines. The ordinary rails were nowhere to be seen.

In spite of it all, the train rushed through at a terrifying speed. If we go on at this pace, I thought, the driver won't be able to stop at Omonia Square. I looked uneasily at my watch. I had five minutes left to make it to an important appointment. Now the woman was whispering rhythmically in my ear: "You are me, I am you, you are me, I am you." Her words copied faithfully the taka-tak-taka-tak rhythm of the train. The speed had now increased, and at its highest, a sort of music broke out, as when a spinning top comes to rest in spasms, while the rotation gradually decreases, and drags itself on the ground with a metallic noise before it falls sideways and stops. The train had reached the station. When I tried to get out, I realized I couldn't lift myself from the tracks. The train was me!

The Tree of Happiness

"A large bright star shines down on me illuminating from above the cypresses the microcosm of an island."

God's three special messengers finally came, foretold by the stars, bearing their precious gifts to the world. I will bless them all my life, because they brought me the water of life, the drink of the gods, the herb of the twilight, the Christmas tree, the stalk of desire, the leaf of enjoyment, the melon field of pleasure, the thousand-times-mentioned all-knowing noodle, the confidential client, the flower of the heart, the super-substantial lentisk shrub, the golden fruit of the cypress, the ugliest beauty, the quintessential mist, the alabaster of the kings, the fleshly charm, the delicious meat, the invisible good, the concealed passion, the convenient lie, the cheek of hope, the sickle of reality, the eyelash of truth, the woman's desire, the tiger in the garden, the remains of paradise, the vaporizers of immortality, the dewdrops of blood, the joy of the bowels, the incurable wound, the golden crown, the tearful glance, the hair-raising caress, the palace of desperation, the blackberry of resurrection, the lion's share, the knife of abundance, the sultan's birthday cake, the little being of the odalisque, the beloved's eyes, the door of immortality.

When the procession drew near and I saw the faces clearly, suddenly I suffered a horrible memory loss.

I had no idea who I was, who was coming, what they were bringing me and why. I couldn't remember anything at all. I was completely stripped of understanding, in the belly of ignorance. Meanwhile they drew near. They arrived and started to speak. At first my ears didn't even work. I didn't hear what they were saying.

Finally the words I could make out were completely meaningless. They echoed inside me like coins falling into an empty cistern, like the rustling of leaves in the wind, the gnashing of teeth, the breaking of waves, the gurgling of a faucet. They were bird calls and animal cries, they were unknown elements that dissolved inside me and broke into a thousand pieces. I was in a strange place where things that once had meaning had now lost it. I was a hole that devoured everything and returned it to the original chaos before the separation into distinct things, before the kingdom of names, before the establishment of ideas.

I was an empty desert. Storms and whirlwinds blew through me. They carried along my earlier thoughts, literally turning them into dust. But the trouble didn't stop there, because after they destroyed every distinct idea, my concepts disintegrated, distorting my words fearfully. Every word was like a cannon. When words reached my ears they took on another sense. The conventional grammatical rules, as when we call a spade a spade, were no longer obeyed. Nouns became birds and fluttered away before my eyes, terrified by some beast lying in wait, behind my brain, to eat them. They became stones and horrible valleys that spread out before me when confronted by the corpses of my meditations.

At other times verbs ran away in my head and turned into liquids, into torrents of rain, into faucets that overflowed inside me and flooded everything. Alternately they scorched me when they touched me and I became their burnt offering, a festering wound. Then they became dirt that people threw and covered me. At first they did it as a joke, but gradually they buried me and I found myself in a tomb of verbs. When I tried to cry out, my words were immediately distorted and took on another meaning. For example, "help" or "get me out of here" turned into "I really don't ever want to see you again."

The misunderstandings increased. Gigantic disagreements made us lose contact. We inhabited unrelated worlds, divided by impassable rivers and enormous gorges that gaped between us without an earthquake, as if the earth were opening to swallow us. We now lived in these gorges. I saw people very high up searching for me with ropes. I kept shouting but of course they didn't hear me. A rope came down but it fell as soon as I tried to pull on it.

My life passed before my eyes as if it were someone else's. I laughed at the ridiculous superstitions and groundless fears of the man I used to be. I saw that up till then I had only two behavior patterns and that I had always spent my time on the edge of an abyss that followed me like a faithful dog. I was programmed to do certain things, to bring about certain acts. But I did them all wrong. Nothing came out right.

Everyone laughed at my expense and I laughed loudest of all. My laughter started to become annoying. It was as if a raging ocean drowned out everything. First all the other sounds disappeared. Then, one by one, the houses, first my own and then the neighboring one, and afterwards whole cities sunk under my laughter, which turned into liquid. Later it began to threaten the mountains, but the influence of the stars saved the situation and just barely averted a new cataclysm.

This escape from the cataclysm created serious external wounds in the human race, which slowly started to die off because of its evil ways and its remorse. Giant shadows replaced the last people. These shadows wrote messages on vertical gashes in the earth using beds of rock as passwords and managed to communicate with one another. But finally the landslides isolated them and wore them out and the false shadows destroyed them. But they soon reappeared on walls, in the passageways, on the windows, on the doors of abandoned houses, huge advertisements for another life that no longer had any living representatives.

In the meantime a third (daily) world war had broken out in the souls of the people. They fought with their delusions. People appeared everywhere who maintained – very reasonably – that there existed eyewitnesses of the psychic dismemberment of China by Russia and America. They represented the systematic annihilation of all bastions of civilization. They had verified the dehydration of the planet and the final armistice took place when the oceans were transformed into drinking water and energy. The psychic disarray from this great catastrophe was so intense that in order to protect the populace from an epidemic of madness, the psychiatrists decided to vaccinate everyone with a new drug, alexitritoparaneurosine.

This drug satisfied mankind's appetite for aggression and destruction with visions so convincing, that the people who took it were certain that they had lived through everything they had experienced under its influence.

In their wildest fantasy, everyone became the Gorilla, the Golem, the King Kong of civilization.

Gigantic disagreements shattered the Lilliputian cities. Monstrous footsteps were left in the steppes of Central Asia, tracks that future generations of scientists, completely perplexed, would study.

The end of the war set the human race free from the nightmare of the sword of Damocles. Fate played an external role as a spiritually advanced humanity grew accustomed to resolve its differences. This cleansing came by means of terror. A feeling of pity developed, like the morning star pouring out its sweet light onto a humanity tamed at last.

When I woke up, I had become a multitude of beings, my individual existence was gone and I saw myself lying in a mausoleum on the mountain where they were foolishly waiting on me. I was the last dead man. In my hands they had placed the magic herb that offered consolation even after death.

As a multitude I lived again in thousands of children, men, and women. I felt all of them as an inseparable part of myself. We were joined together as one organism not only by ordinary means of communication, but also by a sophisticated telepathic network that branched out to everyone like the nervous system.

My thought originated not only from my cells, but also from a constantly shifting ideal point that coordinated every activity automatically.

For example, if a little girl fell and struck her knee, I raised her up without her even knowing it and I brought her where she would get the care she needed. Then I let her return to her play. My control over my limbs was so complete that half the time when they did things we didn't like, I lulled them to sleep so that they could work mechanically without knowing it. I left them on their own only when they were enjoying themselves, doing things they liked, such as reading, watching movies, making love, going for walks, playing games — while those things people once did compelled by law they now do willingly, on their own, so that life became a constant and unending enjoyment from birth to death.

The biggest problem people had was how to catch themselves on the run. Ordinary methods such as railroads or bicycles didn't help, neither for the fugitives themselves nor for those who were chasing them. Finally the old saying "whoever got there first saw the Lord" became all too true, especially when accompanied by generous bribes. No one could operate any other way. The expression "You step on me and I'll step on you" became the law of the land. This resulted in countless innocent victims because of the overcrowding and the inadequacy of public transportation. Silent or vocal protests didn't solve the problem, for people realized these two methods were pointless, considering the stony apathy of the authorities.

The solution, of course, wasn't long in coming. It took the form of a swift new locomotive that served the whole world. It shone like a star and was at once revered and respected by everyone. It was triumphantly applauded on its first journey as the spontaneous ticket of priority, by which the first always gave place to the last. So there was no need to hurry because those who came last were always the first to find a seat.

The inventor of this brilliant means of survival of a ruined way of life killed himself shortly afterward, perhaps out of excessive joy and satisfaction. Soon, however, the oppression started up again, this time in the form of a corrosion that spread over the world, which in other respects was highly polished, at least on the official side. On the other hand, we don't have to concern ourselves with this since that same evening a colleague undertook an exhaustive and erudite investigation into the brick-red color of the fox.

For God's sake, lighten up, have a little understanding of the seriousness of the joke. Think of my remarks about how some people take things too literally and have an urge to tear everything down in order to build castles in the air. Not that the possibility is out of the question, but of course I don't want to be the one who will lead an army through the Daedalean straits of fantasy to the deceptive plains of the Unrealized. I don't want people to impute responsibilities to me after the fact, for chance deviations from the straight and narrow, when they hadn't imposed those responsibilities on me in the first place. That doesn't worry me at all, for what have I to do with the sort of estimates that might turn out one day to be everyone's responsibility?

Some things are now clear. On the one hand there's the half who thinks something suspicious is going on and becomes distrustful and upset over every little thing, and on the other hand, the other half — the blessed and ignorant for whom nothing ever happens and even if something does happen, it has the character of absolute nonexistence. In a situation like that, it's better to advance full speed ahead, knowing full well that some reef will turn up to save the captain's self-esteem.

Progressive Distortion of 16th-Century Oil Painting With Castle Soldier Shepherd and Woman

Emerging from the gate of the central building of the castle's entrance the soldier raises his arm to stop the flight of an arrow being shot from the right side of the spot where he stands travelling toward the eastern battlements of the castle's fort beyond the moat surrounding it where the hillock with the sheep begins and the shepherd stands holding his staff which bears the sculpted head of a dragon whose open mouth contains a replica of the castle with its moat and its fortifications while a tiny soldier raises his ironclad fist in a symbolic gesture on which the arrow breaks its flight while some twenty feet below on the handle of the half-opened gate of the castle's central courtyard the same scene is reenacted, the shepherd now holding the soldier's head beneath his arm wades through the shallow water of the moat, and the arrow is still travelling toward the soft breast of the woman who is hiding in the bushes holding in her arms the decapitated body of the soldier-shepherd while the archer aims at her from the third window of the eastern wing of the castle, the woman's ex-lover whom the shepherd had replaced after he had joined the army some years later and since the time element has progressively distorted the painting and the soldier with the iron glove by the gateway holds up the arrow while the half-naked body of the woman is floating in the moat near the hill with the flock of sheep still holding the head of the decapitated shepherd and the soldier-archer's arrow now stopped somewhere between the shepherd's head and the woman's breast in its rapid flight toward the bark of the only tree in the landscape situated behind, at a small distance from the moat whose castle is now plunged in gloom as the setting sun hides the soldier in a long shadow and the invisible archer on the battlements aims at the flock of sheep which are now in the pen while the little boy closes the door for the night.

The Bride

He brought out his notebook — he was standing on the street corner and furiously taking notes. What he was noting down remained a mystery.

The telegraph.

The bride took off her wedding dress as she came in.

The bride took off her wedding dress and didn't arrive at all. The bride was blown out, the bride was all lit up.

The bride was a candle burning in the countryside.

The bride was bad weather, depression.

The bride was the bride, and only the bride and always the bride.

The bride undressed and went up and down the stairs three times naked and blew out the candle and when she lit it, she let the flame lick her breasts and her ears and behind her ears, in that sensitive spot till her bridal dress caught fire and she opened her gown and produced a stamp and glued it on top of the table with her tongue.

It was a one-hundred drachma stamp — a stamp with no picture on it.

And she took out her breasts and rested them on the floor and up she went and stood on her breasts on the tips of her toes and she took off her hair and spread it out on the window to dry and she took out her eyes and put them in a drawer so they wouldn't get dirty or lost.

And she first unglued one foot, and then the other, and hung them over her head, and with one hand she unscrewed the other hand, so that both were almost ready to fall off her body.

And she grasped her head and took it off as a hat and rested it on the table where she had glued the stamp.

And then she took off all the hairs from her legs one by one and arranged them in front of her head, and she rolled her torso around the hole of her vagina and placed it on the top of a stake that impaled her completely.

And then all these objects dried up and wrinkled and turned into a mist.

The moon on the other hand, less solid than even a cloud, had been the subject of much debate. Was it made of rock or dust? Wasn't it a cloud with holes in it? In consequence, if we touched it, would the full moon become double, then single, and wane and disappear entirely until it reappeared again?

Beautiful bride − you who knew how to take off your legs and grant them to me one at a time − what has become of you? How are you? Where have you gone? Moonlit or in darkness, you hide, you lock yourself up in the closets of the heart. Where am I to look for you now? Am I to open all my closed cupboards to find you? To remember who you are, to see whether your childlike face is still a face or whether it has become a stray piece of dried fruit or so many other things a face can turn into when you neglect it, when you ignore it, when you can't stand it, when you can't do any solid thinking, when, and when, and when... forever, when.

In Praise of Folly

Folly is what we call it. In fact we mean insanity. To be a fool is one thing to be insane is another. My belief in reason as in woman is absolute. It's a must. Without it we are nowhere. For me reason is insane. I have every reason to believe in the insanity of reason. Doctor Lacan knew what he was talking about when he called writing a symptom. It is in reality symptomatic of not being able to. The ground has been sawn off my feet. The sky has been crushed by too much solicitude. Never were two equals less dissimilar than man and his friends the animals. Women must count although they exist. Someone said have fun. Another said have a cigar. Both are good for you. Although I don't recommend them. I'm best known for my lyrical qualities. My reflective strain comes earlier. Later there was neither as in the beginning. But isn't that typical of everyone? So in what do I differ from others? Is my megalomania smaller than theirs? Or my egomania less offensive? I could be both if I had the time and the courage. Happily, I don't lack opportunity. Pleasure is best when it is accompanied by pain. Suffering prepares you for enjoyment. Then the pain returns. Our relation to women is not related to pain. Pain is a pure invention. It has nothing to do with anything. Men and women indifferently are displeased about it. No amount of discipline will cure bad habits. They only become better. To indulge in them raises a problem. The problem of mortality. If only mortality were portable. It would be fun taking the trip. To think is a form of madness. It's more unavoidable than running.

Women are much superior to men. Yet they are equals. No feeling is foolproof. The proof is still deeply buried in the pudding. No amount of strip-mining will extract it without the help of a dentist's assistance. Be reassured no teeth are involved. At least yet. Presentability is all that matters for the time being. Your case although unargued is best seen without too much light. To shed light on something is to strip it of all its mystery. Yet the mystery persists. To be a fool is not easy. To be insane is remarkable. Especially since they are rarely not the same. To be crazy over a woman is not insanity. It's as healthy as a doughnut eaten by a fat man. Or as useful as a safety device thrown overboard for a drowning man. Or as preposterous as serving a cause to the end. Or as refined as the perfume extracted from the testicles of the muskrat.

English Composition 3

It has been raining all day. The doctor cannot come tomorrow. Today is not Friday. It will be Friday in two days. When the rain stops I will go and visit my aunt. My cousin is thirteen and I am eleven. I will probably sleep in my cousin's house for the weekend. Three years later when I was thirteen and she was sixteen we experimented sexually. For a whole month we kissed each other on the mouth to see what it was like. She was the first one to give me the news about menstruation. It was immediately after my father's funeral. The shock made me forget about my father's death. That's when we started experimenting. We continued to experiment for the next three years. By then I was fourteen and she was sixteen. That was the time when I bought my first radio. I'm not afraid of catching the flu. Almost everybody I know is sick with it. My cousin also has the flu. That did not stop us from kissing. The sexual impulse is more powerful than the fear of influenza. Last night the sun was cut to pieces by a very nasty man. The nasty man was punished and the sun was able to come up again. My redheaded German Sudeten governess, Vera Lipenska, God bless her soul, used to hang me up by the hair in order to punish me. Since then I have had a curious attraction for redheads, mixed with repulsion. Some say the sexual impulse is even more powerful than the Czar. The doctor has changed his appointments so that he can come tomorrow although tomorrow is not Friday. There are two discrepancies in the text you have just heard. Has anyone been able to spot them?

Stories About Nothing

I got up in the morning and went to the bathroom. Strictly speaking there was no one there, apart from myself. But then I consider myself less than no one, especially when I'm in the bathroom looking at myself in the mirror about to embark in the dubious operation of shaving the hair off my skin. My facial skin is on the cheeks the jowls and down the throat but not below the Adam's apple. Then as I see myself in the mirror and notice my thinning hair and my white moustache my flesh getting a little flabbier around the jaws, I say to myself trying to convince myself of this truth: Maturity. Now I know everything there is to know. This is not old age. It's wisdom. Or at least its exterior signs. I'm now in full possession of my intellectual powers. At my age others are prime ministers, generals, ambassadors, Nobel prize winners, chairmen of corporations, and professors. This last one rings a bell but it does not impress me. I'm nowhere by being a professor. What I should be is a best-seller. A public figure. A household word. A TV star. Famous at least as Einstein. Or Dorothy Lamour. Or even Hedy Lamar. Jack the Ripper? No not that. That would be too painful for my victims. I'll have to avoid the temptation of crime at all costs. It's the easy way that's more difficult. I never understood why crime is easy, as they say. Easy street, man? No kidding. How do you mug someone? Easy eh? And what about the consequences? We poets have a way about us. Perpetual dreamers of all kinds of crazy things. Never moving a little finger to do anything about it. Write about it yes. Anything shocking and startling. To disturb, confuse, make people feel at a loss. To startle to frighten away. To alienate. To anguish. All this is part of the program to reassure. To console. To gladden. To entertain. To amuse. To provoke the rare emotions of sadness nostalgia and despair. To evoke. Faces events and things. Autumn clouds. Seasons. Death. Love. Leaves falling. People going to work. People returning from work. The passage of time. Clichés clichés, like old age and youth. Realities but also clichés. To be loved to be unloved. No wonder I'm not a best-seller. I don't believe in myself. I'm not bored enough to be Beckett. I don't hate enough to be Joyce or Dante. And I'm not even amused enough to be Ionesco. Ugh. Too much disgust is in me. So what am I going to be if it's not too late? Well nothing, whispers the voice. Better be nothing and take it easy than something and go through hell. See how reassuring I am? Be nothing be nothing be nothing. . . . Soothing isn't it? I could play this record all day and never tire of it. Be nothing it's really something.

Small Contribution to the Windmill Series

Don Quixote attacking the windmills with a shield-mirror on which is reflected the windmill which also has a mirror which reflects Don Quixote attacking the windmill with a shield-mirror where is reflected the windmill attacked by Don Quixote etc:

or

Don Quixote with a shield representing Don Quixote on his horse who bears a shield with Don Quixote represented on his horse

this first Don Quixote is a painting of him, sitting in his armchair, reflected in a mirror into which Don Quixote gazes, which is the illustration of a book that a child sitting next to him looks at while the real Don Quixote leans over him in full armor with an amused look on his face examining the illustration of himself sitting in an armchair with a child by his side reading a book, which is a scene in a picture in the Palace of the Doges hanging at the far end of the dining hall and is being observed by an assembly of people among whom one distinguishes the familiar figure of Don Quixote himself amused by the sight of himself in a picture and which is but a description that a German princess is reading in a Bavarian castle, which is itself a scene of a Restoration play in England representing a German heroine reading and which play is described by a young man to another in a tavern in which we distinguish Don Quixote drinking in the background listening to what the young men are talking about, which is no less than an episode in Cervantes' book on Don Quixote considered apocryphal in which a young girl is reading in her bed and falls in love with Don Quixote who, she imagines, opens the door and enters the room to make love to her, since she is no other than the Dulcinea, the real one, reading this story some years after Don Quixote's death — the real one's and of whose existence she had been unaware until then, an episode which one can find in the memoirs of one, Don Quixote's neighbor, named Sancho Panza, which are exhibited in the Don Quixote museum in the little town in the province of La Mancha, which visitors are examining with care, under the painting number one hanging from the wall with the shield-mirror that a photographer is photographing to reproduce in a popular magazine while he is himself reflected in the mirror of the shield while taking the photo a young girl is going to see soon, she herself being a descendant of Don Quixote from his sister (did she exist?) and who will identify herself to her supposed ancestor by adding her face to the painting of Don Quixote sitting in his room in the castle in his armchair.

Language or Silence?

I have to admit language drives me crazy. The more I think of it the more I'm positive that it's language that's responsible for everything that goes wrong with me. It's the way I put it. It's my diction. My vocabulary. My grammar. My syntax. My sentences. My pronouns. My nouns. My adjectives. All in the wrong place. All displaced and deconstructed and misconstrued in my mind. To hell with language. It should be banned. We should go back to signs. After all the fish do well enough without it, and so do birds, although they have the lamentable tendency to sing sometimes, and beasts growl and grunt and bark and miaou and hiss, but even without all this, silently they go about their business quite effectively. I'm for the new silence. No more words. No more speech. Silent teaching. Films. Images. Gestures that explain everything. Looks. Glances that talk a million words a second. A reproachful look from one I love can last me for all eternity. I know we all know these things. But we forget them. Let's refresh our memory then and forget language. Once and forever let's return to the Caves of Silence and stop our ears to any babble, even the speech of the wind and the waves. So when the supreme judge asks you out of the blue: LANGUAGE OR SILENCE, don't answer anything. He'll understand.

Where Does The Spirit
Of Your Poetry Reside?

The spirit of my poetry resides near the Tuamoto islands. It
moves freely along the lines of the changing winds. From island
to island all kinds of chiefs give me the latest in spirit lore. On
one of the islands, the Chief shows me a hole in the ground near
a cave, which he claims communicates directly with the other
world. This tunnel is also connected to ancient Greece. Indeed,
as I dared to go into it a little way, I met a couple of soldiers
wearing helmets crested with horsetails. What they spoke
sounded more like Persian than Greek. They had a very strong
drawl. Yarooo awdrawoul yorl arouwahau . . . Perhaps the
conditions of the other world had corrupted their classical accent.
In fact they sounded very much like my local informants. Could
it all be a masquerade? The thought has occurred to me before,
that history is in reality a huge masquerade. Nations disguising
themselves in various clothes, uniforms, costumes, for the
occasion. The battles are mainly sham and all is prearranged, as
ethnic groups surrender the running of history to other groups.
There is no truth behind history. It's all pretend. Even languages
are invented on the spur of the moment and then forgotten.
That's why it's so hard to reconstruct them. Only those who have
kept on repeating and learning by heart their old roles have been
able to preserve anything worthwhile mentioning. For instance
the Tuamoto islanders were once cast in the role of Aetolians.
They have long since forgotten their ancient history. What
remains are these two soldiers in a tunnel which they exhibit

with pride. You might then conclude that the spirit of my poetry resides where it resides. There's no specific scene that I prefer more than any other. Besides, I'm only moved by the spurious. By what is late, imitative, and grossly exaggerated. I have no time to waste on original masterpieces. They are just good models for others to mold themselves on.

Advice to a Young Poet

Nothing is more loved by life than life itself. It can also be
most hated. These two form a pair of harmonious opposites. No
coincidentia this. When I was young I was more handsome than
now. But now since I am more intelligent than young, I'm also
handsome. Which makes me a loser on both counts. You never
win when you win. It's only a foretaste of future defeat. To win
now is to lose later. To win later is to lose now. My love of
sophistry is only equalled by my sophistry of love. I'd go to any
lengths to twist around an argument on love in favor of my
opponent. Poetry without thought is like thought without poetry.
Both are as dismal as they are profitable. Styles must be forgotten
as quickly as they are learned. In order to forget them they must
not be easily remembered. To write is to unlearn how not to
write. Please don't take me seriously, I was only joking. But then
it's only when I'm not joking that I'm serious. Never believe what
your elders tell you. Only trust those who are the same age as
you are. Even they can be misleading you if they are not lying.
Confusion is the worst example for the best of purposes. There
is no purpose in example. Therefore confusion has arisen. Various
purposes do not create any more confusion than necessary.
Thank god for that at least. What would we be without it?
Nothing more than we are now. Don't laugh, it's disrespectful to
God. How many times have I laughed at creation without
regretting it. I now regret having laughed so much without
regretting it. To regret is not to laugh at something. If before and

83

after the act there was as much remorse as during the course of it, there would be less to be angry about, but more to grind your teeth on. I'm very entertained by strange corpses among stars as all astronomers predict. Alas I can't do anything about it. It's all too much for me, which comes to less and less. My total commitment on how to write is very moving to others. To me it is only laughable. For as much as I despise *ignorance*, I hate to *know*. If I puzzle you, you must be pleased. There is nothing more gratifying than being puzzled. I have no other advice to give except on what has not yet been said. So my final word is: Don't write. Even if you have to write at all costs, even if your life depends on it. It's far better to be what you are. Sincerely. Dramatically. To the end of your most profitable life. So don't listen to any other voice except your own. And that too with caution. Be as brazen as you can be deceptive. As honest as you may without being reflective. Throw hesitation down the drain and buy yourself a typewriter. Without it no writer can call himself or herself an orphan.

What Poetry Means To Me

I believe that poetry is a very archaic manner of speaking, intimately connected with the word. It would be impossible to conceive of the world without images. The world is like a city built with bricks of colored letters. Mainly, the color of these bricks is earth red. In other words, my only objection is that poetry, though not usually food for thought, is a lot more than we need, since many of our words are fulfilled without the poetry of poetry for poetry. All our cupboards are not only cluttered up with meaningless phrases but also with clothes and shoes that are out of fashion. Poetry has a very strange effect on children. It makes them look clean and eat less. Wolves, I am told, go to town on poetry. They use it as snow. Love poetry, although very different from the love of poetry, does not disturb me at all. I like it. I like it. Dante believed in the theology of love (or the love of theology), Byron liberated the Maid of Athens from her demon lovers. Wordsworth, Keats and Co. formed a brilliant closed circle worthy of attention. Nonsense equals NON-SENSE. My love of coffee is closest and the furthest removed from my love of "blackness." I cherish "black thoughts" in a cup of Turkish coffee. Poetry is what helps the living to die and the dead to live. Both are to each other what they are to me: distant relatives. Having lived all my life in the arms of poetry, I now cherish her in my arms. I distribute it to those who don't care about life any more (they are usually unready for it) whatever life they like to think about most, *almost endlessly.*

My Afterlife Guaranteed

Can I go on writing after death? I have written in the middle of electrical storms, on the eve of death, and before the ship went down, I have sung on the decks, and when the pillars crumbled, I was in the temple, striking my vocal chords with my last breath...I wrote during total blackouts and breakdowns. When trapped underground without air. Before the firing squad of dictatorships...I even wrote during rock concerts and when asleep in my own bed. All I need now is pen and paper, and I'll go on writing forever.

Yet how will I find pen and paper in the grave?

Hmm. I hadn't thought of that. I'll have to order it beforehand. And in great quantities. But what if it rots?

Then I'll have to write with a spirit pen on spiritual paper. Or even better, I'll dictate to some living poet I'll inhabit after my death. After all, the blind Milton dictated to his daughter what he had seen in the night of the next portion of *Paradise Lost*, and Fergus McRoich recited the *Tain* from his tomb, and Homer appealed to the Muses to help him out, and Shakespeare's "Thought went along with His Hand," as the Players tell us. And Blake, ah yes Blake believe it or not wrote his *Milton* from portions of an immense poem existing elsewhere, and the *Mahabarata* was dictated by Vyasa from memory to the God of

86

writing himself, the Elephant-form Ganesha, and Aristeas wrote "The Arismaspea" after he had returned from the dead. And Dante made the same journey, "nel mezzo del cammin," of his life, and Er the Pamphylian according to Plato described the Other World in great detail, and all those shamans from Central Asia who journeyed to the other world and could tell their audience where they were all along, and Odysseus returning from the other world after ten years, and then going off again to pay further debts incurred, and last but not least Yeats, who took down "A Vision" from spirits inhabiting his wife in a trance. . . . And me writing my "Anonymous Poem of Photeinos Ayannis" after two puffs on a powerful joint which put me in contact with the poet my great grandfather, and Ginsberg who heard Blake's voice and wrote "Kaddish" for him, and for his mother, both dead, and the Spirit of Mescal helping Castaneda to under-stand . . . and Poe writing, under the spirit of Opium, and Rimbaud writing "A Season in Hell" during a serious illness when he thought he had died, and Breton consulting the mediums about automatic writing, and Andrei Siniavski, inhabited by all those spirits when he wrote the *Fantastic Stories* and *Liubimov*, and Jung who saw his Guru while in a coma, and Reich, who inhabited Makaveieff and made him shoot the film, *Mysteries of the Organism*, and Joyce, who could not help distorting every English sentence he heard through his lifetime, and Beckett, whose characters continue to be immersed in writing after death, and Meyrinck who wrote *The Golem* from the point of view of a man without memory, and Bulgakov who wrote *The Master and Margarita* after Goethe, and Dylan Thomas writing about the haunted dead in Wales. . . .

All these people went far beyond their own lives and saw into the future and into the past what no one had yet seen, as I saw the secret of the *Iliad* and *Odyssey* as they were conceived by Homer. And think of Socrates dictated to by his daemon, inhabiting Plato after his death and making him write all those dialogues . . . about *himself*!

Have I convinced you Mr. Man in the Street?

Man in the Street: You've convinced me about writing after death. But that's no big deal. What about sex after death? . . .

Not a bad idea. I'll have to think about it. But I can tell you immediately that according to Apollinaire, Louis the II of Bavaria, the "Moon King" as he was known, had succeeded in sleeping with every dead beauty he could think of, thanks to a miraculous machine. . . .

Man in the Street: Where's that machine now?

Me: Lost somewhere in the mountains of Bavaria.

Man in the Street: Let's go dig it up man . . .